Listen · Read · Think

SCIENCE

Volcanoes and Earthquakes

Gina Nuttall

Teacher Created Resources

Copyright © QEB Publishing, Inc. 2004

Published in the United States by
QEB Publishing, Inc.
23062 La Cadena Drive
Laguna Hills, CA 92653

This edition published by
Teacher Created Resources, Inc.
6421 Industry Way
Westminster, CA 92683

www.teachercreated.com

Library of Congress Control Number 2004102035

ISBN 978-1-4206-8121-5

Written by Gina Nuttall
Designed by Zeta Jones
Editor Hannah Ray
Picture Researcher Joanne Beardwell

Series Consultant Anne Faundez
Creative Director Louise Morley
Editorial Manager Jean Coppendale

Printed and bound in China

Picture credits
Key: t = top, b = bottom, c = center, l = left, r = right
Corbis Bettman 16 /Yann Arthus-Bertrand 12 /Lloyd Cluff 14 /Roger Ressmeyer 5 /Galen Rowell 13 /Douglas Peebles 9 /Jim Sugar 6; **Gettyimages** John T. Barr Contributor 11b /Ralph Crane Stringer 11t /Bill Greenblatt 18 /Keystone Staff 10t /Salah Malkawi Stringer 17 /Phil Mislinski Stringer 10b/ Art Wolfe 4; **NASA** 13t

Contents

Volcanoes and earthquakes

Why does a mountain suddenly explode?

Why does the ground shake and make buildings fall?

Scientists know the answer:

The surface, or **crust**, of the Earth is like a jigsaw puzzle. It is made up of different pieces of rock. Sometimes the pieces bump into each other.

This is when volcanoes and earthquakes can happen.

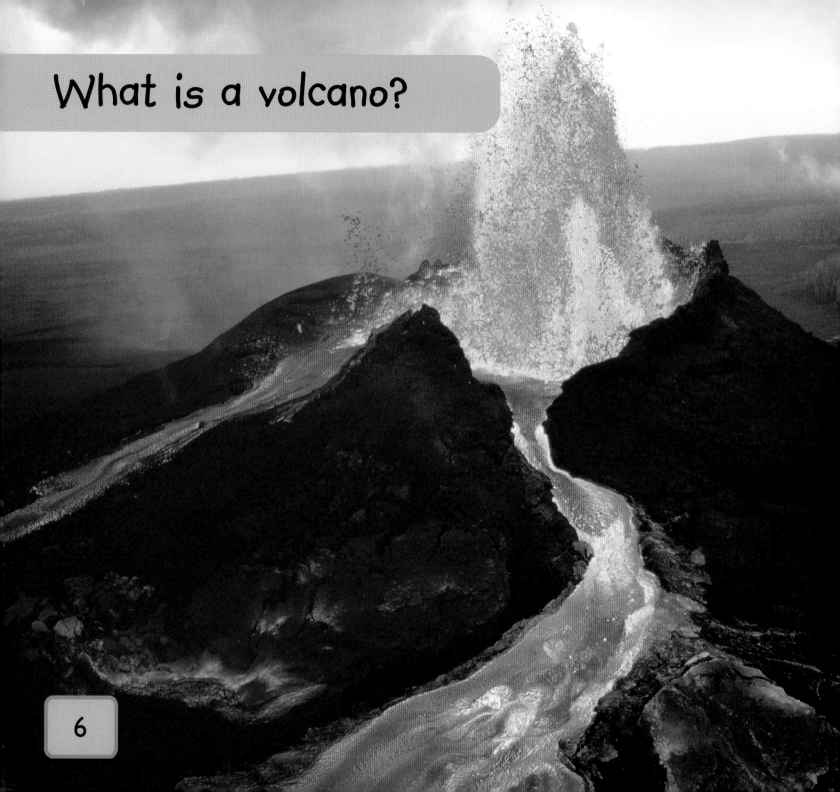

What is a volcano?

A volcano is a mountain that blows its top!

Some of the rock under the Earth's surface is so hot that it melts. This melted rock is called **magma**.

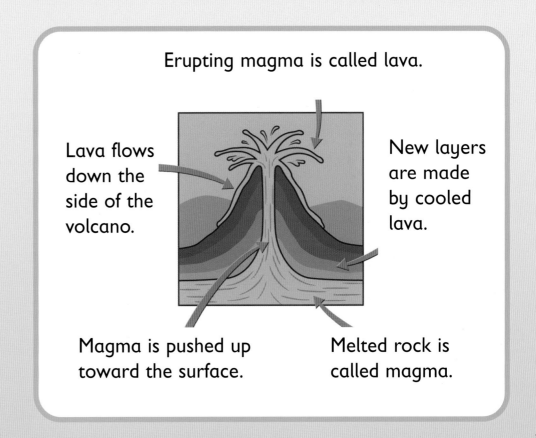

Erupting magma is called lava.

Lava flows down the side of the volcano.

New layers are made by cooled lava.

Magma is pushed up toward the surface.

Melted rock is called magma.

Sometimes magma is pushed up to the surface.
It explodes, or **erupts**, out of the ground.
The hot rock that pours out is called **lava**.

When the lava cools, it makes a new layer of rock.
Volcanoes become bigger every time they erupt.

Different types of volcano

There are many volcanoes on Earth.
There are more than 500 active volcanoes.
An active volcano is one that still erupts.

Some volcanoes are quiet, but they could
erupt again one day. They are called
dormant volcanoes.

Very old volcanoes will never erupt again.
They are called extinct volcanoes.

This extinct volcano is in Hawaii.
It is called the Punchbowl Crater.

Volcanoes around the world

Vesuvius

Mount Vesuvius is a volcano in Italy. It erupted a long time ago and buried the whole city of Pompeii under dust and ash.

Kilauea

The volcano Kilauea erupted in Hawaii in 1983. The lava did not stop flowing for twenty years!

Mount Etna

Mount Etna in Italy is one of the world's most active volcanoes. It has been erupting for over half a million years.

Mount St. Helens

This beautiful mountain in Washington State was dormant for more than 100 years. Then, in 1980, it erupted violently.

Volcanoes are everywhere

Volcanoes can erupt under water, as well as on land. New islands can grow from the cooled lava.

Surtsey Island is an island off the coast of Iceland. It was made by a volcano.

There are even volcanoes on the moon and other planets.

The largest volcano in our solar system is Olympus Mons on Mars.

It is almost three times higher than Mount Everest, the highest mountain on Earth.

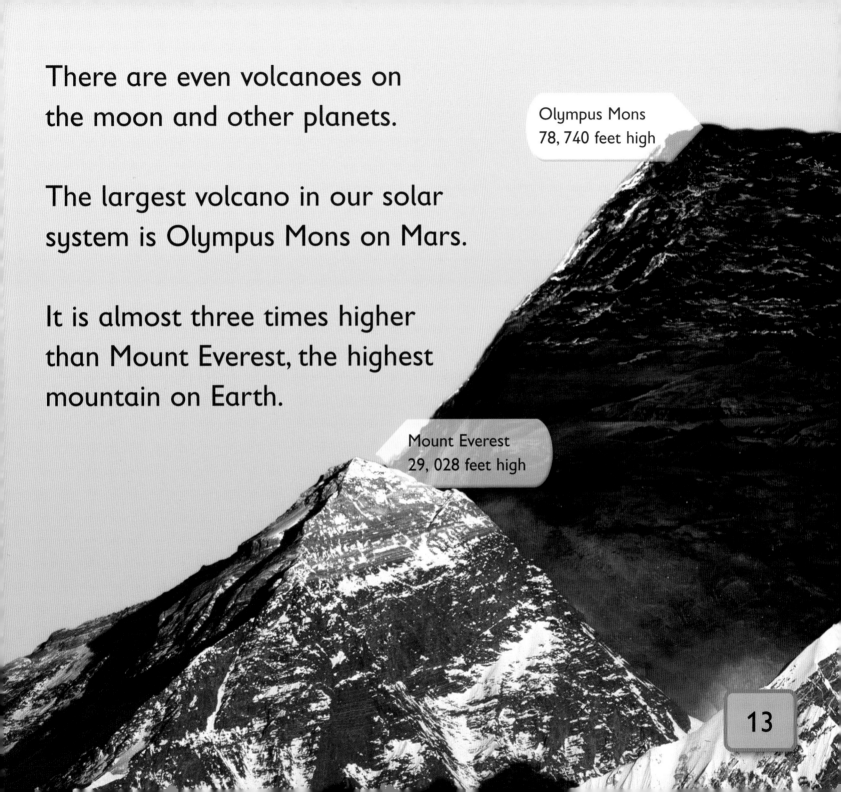

Olympus Mons
78, 740 feet high

Mount Everest
29, 028 feet high

What are earthquakes?

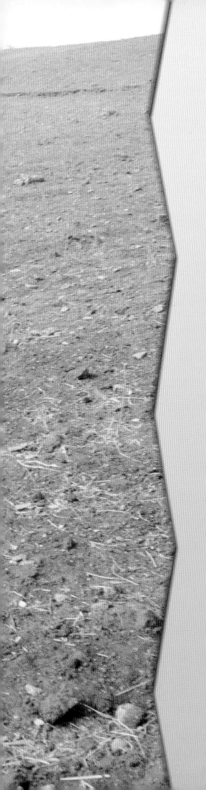

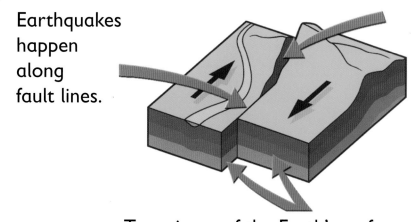

Earthquakes happen along fault lines.

The line between the pieces is called a fault line.

Two pieces of the Earth's surface.

Earthquakes happen when the Earth's surface shakes and cracks.

Tiny earthquakes happen almost every day. This is because the puzzle pieces of the Earth's surface are always moving.

Earthquakes happen along the edges of the pieces in the Earth's crust. The edges are called fault lines.

Earthquakes around the world

Earthquakes happen all over the world.

**California:
San Francisco, 1906**
This massive earthquake lasted only about 40 seconds, but it was very strong. Huge cracks appeared in the roads. Many buildings in this big city fell. This caused fires, which destroyed many more buildings.

The remains of a house after the earthquake in Bam.

Iran: Bam, 2003

Bam is a very old city.

Many of the buildings were made from mud brick.

The earthquake destroyed most of them.

Measuring earthquakes

The strength of an earthquake can be measured.

Scientists use a machine called a **seismograph**.

The measurement is called the Richter scale.

A scientist checking a seismograph.

The Richter Scale

8 Whole cities are destroyed.

7 Ground cracks. Whole buildings fall down.

6 Walls fall down.

5 Furniture moves about. Buildings are damaged.

4 Felt by lots of people. Walls crack.

3 Feels like a truck going past.

2 Usually cannot be felt by people.

1 Cannot be felt by people.

19

Be prepared

What to do if there is an earthquake:

- Keep calm!

- If you are indoors, drop to the ground. Then you won't fall down.

- Take cover under a table or desk.

- Hold onto a table or desk leg.

- If you are outside, move away from buildings, street lights, and overhead wires.

Always have these things handy:

 *Shoes:* Wear them so you don't hurt yourself on broken objects.

 *Battery-operated flashlight:* Use it if the electricity is cut off.

 *Whistle:* Blow it so someone can find you in the dark.

Glossary

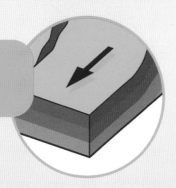

crust—the surface of the Earth.

erupts—when a volcano explodes.

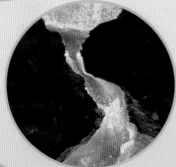

lava—the hot, liquid rock that pours out of a volcano.

magma—very hot rock that has melted.

seismograph—an instrument for measuring earthquakes.

Index

Parents' and teachers' notes

- After reading, look back at the two questions on page 5. Help your child write two- or three-sentence answers to each question. Your child could make drawings to illustrate his/her writing.
- Ask your child to think of words connected to volcanoes and earthquakes. They can be fact words, such as "erupt" or "lava," or words about how volcanoes and earthquakes make him/her feel, such as "amazed" or "scared." Write the words under the headings "Fact Words" and "Feeling Words."
- Talk about the purpose of a glossary (tells the reader the meaning of words in the text) and an index (tells the reader on which pages to find something). Play a game based on information in the glossary and index, such as "What does 'lava' mean?" or "Which page would you look at to find out about fault lines?"
- Make a crossword puzzle or word search for your child using the words in the glossary.
- Ask your child to pretend he/she has seen a volcanic eruption or has experienced an earthquake. Can he/she write to a friend, telling him/her all about it?

- Ask your child questions, such as "Do you feel any different about volcanoes and earthquakes after reading this book?," "What surprised you most?," "What questions would you still like to ask?," or "Where do you think we can find the answers?"
- Together, find out about some recent earthquakes and volcanic eruptions. Help your child make notes about each one.
- Use a globe or atlas to find the places where some of the volcanoes and earthquakes mentioned in the book can be found.
- Together, make a volcano out of paper. On one side, show the inside, and on the other side of the paper, show the outside. Label the picture.
- Demonstrate how an earthquake causes things to fall down. Make some jello in a pan. When set, place some objects representing houses, trees, electricity wires, and people on the jello. Shake the pan and see what happens.
- Take a walk around your home and identify places that could be dangerous in an earthquake. Make a list. Talk about how you could make your home safer.